FARMSTAND FAVORITES

Honey

Over 75 Farm Fresh Recipes

Farmstand Favorites: Honey
Text copyright © 2012 Hatherleigh Press

Hatherleigh Press is committed to preserving and protecting the natural resources of the Earth. Environmentally responsible and sustainable practices are embraced within the company's mission statement.

Hatherleigh Press is a member of the Publishers Earth Alliance, committed to preserving and protecting the natural resources of the planet while developing a sustainable business model for the book publishing industry.

This book was edited and designed in the village of Hobart, New York. Hobart is a community that has embraced books and publishing as a component of its livelihood. There are several unique bookstores in the village. For more information, please visit www.hobartbookvillage.com.

www.hatherleighpress.com

DISCLAIMER
This book offers general cooking and eating suggestions for educational purposes only. In no case should it be a substitute nor replace a healthcare professional. Consult your healthcare professional to determine which foods are safe for you and to establish the right diet for your personal nutritional needs.

Library of Congress Cataloging-in-Publication Data is available upon request.
ISBN: 978-1-57826-406-3

All Hatherleigh Press titles are available for bulk purchase, special promotions, and premiums. For information about reselling and special purchase opportunities, please call 1-800-528-2550 and ask for the Special Sales Manager.

Cover Design by Nick Macagnone
Interior Design by Nick Macagnone
Cover Photography by Catarina Astrom

Printed in the United States
10 9 8 7 6 5 4 3 2 1

Acknowledgments

Hatherleigh Press would like to extend a special thank you to Jo Brielyn—without your hard work and creativity this book would not have been possible.

Table of Contents

All About Honey

Honey, often dubbed nature's sweetener, is exactly that—a natural, healthy replacement for processed, refined sugar. The honey-making process is a unique procedure created solely by nature, and one that cannot be duplicated by man without the help of honey bees. The sweet substance, which serves as a tasty alternative to white sugar, is created by honey bees when they collect nectar from plants. As 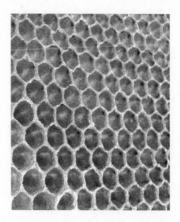 bees carry the nectar in their mouths and return to their hives, a chemical reaction occurs between the nectar and the enzymes in the bees' mouths, turning the nectar into honey. The bees then deposit the honey into the cells of the hives, where it sits until ready. The final step in the process occurs when the honey bees fly around in their hives. The fluttering of their tiny wings offers the ventilation needed to remove moisture from the honey, bringing it to the right consistency for consumption.

Honey that is taken from the honey comb for human use and consumption (also called extracted honey), is generally removed by straining, filtering, or methods that use gravity or centrifugal force. Once the honey is extracted, it is processed and used in various types. You will find honey at your local farmstand or farmers market in these recognizable forms:

Liquid honey: Liquid honey is honey that has no visible crystals in it.

Crystallized honey: Crystallized honey is honey that is granulated and in solid form. Crystallized honey is processed into different forms, such as candied or creamed honey.

Candied honey is hard candy that is filled with honey.

Creamed honey is crystallized honey that has been processed through a method that uses controlled temperature to create a creamy texture similar to peanut butter.

Partially crystallized honey: Partially crystallized honey is a mixture of liquid and crystallized honey.

Comb honey: Comb honey is honey in its natural form. It is the honey served still inside of the honeycomb. Even the beeswax comb itself is edible.

Cut Comb: Cut comb honey is a combination of chunks of honey comb and liquid honey in the jar. Cut comb is also referred to as a liquid-cut comb combination.

Although bees use the same process to make all honey, the colors, aromas, and flavors of honey vary greatly depending on the blossoms from which the bees gather the nectar. Some varieties are almost colorless, while others can be dark shades of brown. In much the same way, the flavors of honey can range from delicate to very bold. Generally, the lighter shades of honey are milder in taste and the darker-colored varieties possess stronger flavors. You can even find types of honey with floral and fruity flavors to them.

Honey color is measured on a scale called a Pfund scale. The scale is a calibrated glass wedge containing amber honey that has a metric ruler on it. The honey sample is placed in a glass trough and is measured in millimeters according to where it lines up with the amber honey. The Pfund scale starts at 0 mm (which is colorless) and ends at 140 mm (which is black).

The U.S. Department of Agriculture (USDA) classifies honey into seven distinct categories:

- **Water White:** Honey that is water white is virtually colorless and resembles water. It measures 8 mm or less on the Pfund scale.

- **Extra White:** Honey that is extra white is darker than water white, but not darker than extra white. Extra white honey measures greater than 8 mm and up to and including 17 mm on the Pfund scale.

- **White:** Honey that is classified as white is darker than extra white but not darker than white. It measures greater than 17 mm and up to and including 34 mm on the Pfund scale.

- **Extra Light Amber:** Honey that is extra light amber is darker than white but not darker than extra light amber. Extra light amber honey measures greater than 34 mm and up to and including 50 mm on the Pfund scale.

- **Light Amber:** Honey that is light amber is darker than extra light amber but not darker than light amber. It measures greater than 50 mm and up to and including 85 mm on the Pfund scale.

- **Amber:** Honey that is classified as amber is darker than light amber but not darker than amber. It measures greater than 85 mm and up to and including 114 mm on the Pfund scale.

- **Dark Amber:** Honey that is classified as dark amber is darker than amber. Dark amber honey is any honey that measures over 114 mm on the Pfund scale.

When selecting honey at your local farmstand or farmers market, keep in mind that there are different grades of honey as well. Honey is classified as one of three quality grades: Grade A, Grade B, and Grade C. The grades, first established by the USDA back in 1985, are determined based on the honey's clarity, aroma, flavor, absence of defects, and water content.

Grade A honey is extracted honey that scores a minimum of 90 out of 100 points on the grading scale based on the determinants mentioned above.

Grade B honey must receive a minimum of 80 points.

Grade C honey scores at least 70 of 100 points. Any honey that receives less than 70 points on the scale is considered substandard grade.

Did you know?

- Honey is 1 to 1.5 times sweeter than sugar.
- A hive of honey bees must fly more than 55,000 miles and tap about 2 million flowers in order to produce one pound of honey.
- The less water content found in honey, the better the quality of it.
- The U.S. Department of Agriculture (USDA) estimates that there are about 2.68 million honey-producing bee colonies in America.
- One tablespoon of honey contains 64 calories and 17 grams of carbohydrates.
- Honey contains antioxidants that fight cholesterol and have the potential to protect against heart disease.
- Darker honeys usually have higher antioxidant content than lighter honeys do.
- Honey is fat-free and cholesterol-free!
- An average worker bee makes $\frac{1}{12}$ of a teaspoon of honey in its lifetime.
- On average, each person in America consumes around 1.3 pounds of honey each year.

Health Benefits of Honey

Honey is a source for many minerals, including calcium, copper, iron, magnesium, manganese, phosphorus, potassium, sodium, and zinc. Vitamins such as B6, thiamin, niacin, riboflavin, pantothenic acid, and certain amino acids are also found in honey.

Honey is a delicious alternative to white sugar and is an excellent source of carbohydrates. It consists of roughly 80 percent natural sugar (mostly fructose and glucose), 18 percent water, and 2 percent minerals, vitamins, pollen, and protein.

Since honey is a natural source of carbohydrates, it is an excellent way to boost energy levels. In fact, it is often used by athletes to boost performance and reduce muscle fatigue during exercise. The glucose found in honey is a natural sugar that the body absorbs quickly, so it provides a quick boost of energy. Fructose, the other main natural sugar found in honey, is absorbed into the body more slowly and provides sustained energy.

The presence of antioxidants and antimicrobial properties in honey are beneficial to the digestive system, can be useful in killing certain bacteria, and can help fight diseases. It is also believed to provide some protection against cancer. Honey has also been used over the centuries in home remedies for cuts and burns, sore throats, weight loss, and cleansing treatments.

The components found in honey help with the metabolism and breakdown of unwanted cholesterol and fatty acid in the organs and tissues, therefore working to fight obesity. Plus, honey has no fat and is cholesterol-free!

Swiss Muesli

Ingredients:
1½ cups rolled oats
1½ cups water
2 cups shredded, unpeeled apples
1½ cups (approximately 9 ounces) pitted prunes, whole or halved
2 tablespoons honey
2 tablespoons lemon juice
½ teaspoon cinnamon
3 bananas, sliced
3 oranges, segmented
1 cup chopped almonds
Plain yogurt or milk (optional)

Directions:
Combine oats, water, shredded apples, prunes, honey, lemon juice, and cinnamon. Cover and refrigerate overnight. In the morning, spoon some of the mixture into a cereal bowl. Top with bananas, oranges, and almonds (or your choice of fresh fruits and nuts). Serve with a dollop of plain yogurt or milk, if desired. Muesli can be stored in a covered container in the refrigerator for several days.

Apple-Honey Oatmeal

Ingredients:

⅔ cup rolled oats

2 cups boiling water

½ teaspoon salt

6 medium-sized apples

1 cup water

¼ cup honey

Directions:

Stir the rolled oats into a pot of boiling water with ½ teaspoon salt and cook them until they thicken. Place the oats in a double boiler and cook for 2 to 4 hours. Pare, core, and slice the apples. Cook the apples in a syrup made of the water and honey until they are soft, but not soft enough to fall apart. To serve, put a large spoonful of the cooked oats in each dish and arrange apple slices on top of the oats. Pour a small amount of the syrup left from cooking the apples over the top and serve immediately.

Note: You may also speed up this process by using quick oats instead of rolled oats.

Avocado Melon Breakfast Smoothie

Fruits & Veggies—More Matters® recipes appear courtesy of Produce for Better Health Foundation (PBH). This recipe meets Centers for Disease Control & Prevention's (CDC) strict nutrition guidelines as a healthy recipe. Find this recipe and others like it online at www.FruitsAndVeggiesMoreMatters.org.

Ingredients:

1 ripe, fresh avocado

1 cup honeydew melon chunks (about 1 slice)

Juice from ½ lime (1½ teaspoons lime juice)

1 cup (8 ounces) fat-free milk

1 cup fat-free plain yogurt

½ cup apple juice or white grape juice

1 tablespoon honey

Directions:

Cut avocado in half, remove pit. Scoop out flesh, place in blender. Add remaining ingredients; blend well. Serve cold. Keeps well in the refrigerator for up to 24 hours. If made ahead, stir gently before pouring into glasses.

Sweet Bananas and Cottage Cheese

Ingredients:

1 banana, sliced
½ cup low-fat cottage cheese
2 teaspoons honey
2 tablespoons granola, optional

Directions:

Cut the banana into long, thin slices. Layer them on the plate and scoop the cottage cheese in the center. Drizzle the honey over the cottage cheese and bananas. Top with the granola, if desired, and serve cold.

Note: For a variation on this recipe, replace the low-fat cottage cheese with low-fat plain yogurt.

Flaxseed and Blueberry Pancakes

Courtesy of American Institute for Cancer Research (AICR)
www.aicr.org

Ingredients:

¾ cup buckwheat flour
¾ cup whole-wheat flour
2 tablespoons ground flaxseed
2 teaspoons baking powder
1 teaspoon baking soda
½ teaspoon salt
1 cup skim or low-fat buttermilk

¾ cup fat-free milk
2 large eggs
1 tablespoon canola oil
1 tablespoon honey
2 cups blueberries, rinsed and set aside
Nonstick cooking spray
Pure maple syrup, to taste

Directions:

In a large bowl, combine flours, flaxseed, baking powder, baking soda and salt. In a separate bowl, mix together buttermilk, milk, eggs, oil, and honey. Pour egg mixture into dry ingredients and stir just until batter is lightly mixed together. (If the batter appears too thick, add a dollop more of milk to thin.) Lumps are okay and over-mixing makes for hard pancakes. Fold in blueberries.

Preheat a large skillet over medium heat. Spray skillet with cooking spray. Use about ¼ cup of batter for each pancake. Cook for about 2 to 3 minutes per side on medium or medium-high heat. The pancakes are ready to flip when bubbles start to appear. Turn over only once and when golden brown. You will have enough for 4 to 6 generous servings, and any leftovers can be frozen for a mid-week treat. Serve with pure maple syrup, to taste.

Cornmeal Pancakes with Honey Fruit Sauce

Courtesy of the National Honey Board

Ingredients:

Fruit Sauce:
1 cup orange juice
1 apple, pared, cored and diced
1 pear, pared, cored and diced
⅓ cup honey
1 teaspoon grated orange peel
1 tablespoon cornstarch
¼ cup water

Cornmeal Pancakes:
½ cup flour
½ cup cornmeal
3 teaspoons baking powder
½ teaspoon salt
1 cup milk
1 egg
3 tablespoons honey
3 tablespoons butter or margarine, melted

Directions:

Fruit Sauce:

Combine orange juice, apple, pear, honey and orange peel in medium saucepan. Bring mixture to boil, reduce heat, and simmer 8 to 10 minutes or until fruits are tender. Dissolve cornstarch in water. Stir into hot mixture; cook and stir until mixture comes to a boil; simmer 1 minute. Makes 2⅓ cups.

Cornmeal Pancakes:

Combine flour, cornmeal, baking powder, and salt in medium bowl; mix well and set aside. Combine milk, egg, honey, and melted butter in small bowl; mix well. Pour liquid mixture into flour mixture; stir only until moistened (batter will be lumpy). Pour about ¼ cup batter for each pancake in hot skillet or on griddle over medium-low heat; cook until bubbles form on surface and edges become dry. Turn and cook 2 minutes longer or until golden. Serve with Fruit Sauce. Makes 8 pancakes.

Honey French Toast

Ingredients:
2 eggs, slightly beaten
¼ cup honey
¼ cup milk
¼ teaspoon salt
6-8 slices bread

Directions:
Blend the eggs, honey, milk, and salt in a medium-sized mixing bowl. Dip a slice of bread in mixture, coat well, and fry on a greased (or buttered) griddle until it is golden brown. Serve French toast immediately with liquid honey, creamed honey, or butter. Blend the eggs, honey, milk, and salt in a medium-sized mixing bowl. Dip a slice of bread in mixture, coat well, and fry on a greased (or buttered) griddle until it is golden brown. Serve French toast immediately with liquid honey, creamed honey, or butter.

Honey Bran Muffins

Ingredients:
1 cup flour
½ teaspoon baking soda
½ teaspoon salt
2 cups bran
½ cup honey
1 tablespoon margarine, melted
1½ cups milk
¾ cup walnuts, chopped, optional

Directions:
Sift together the flour, baking soda, and salt. Blend in the bran. Add the remaining ingredients and mix well. If walnuts are desired, stir them in at this time. Scoop mixture into greased muffin tins or paper liners. Bake at 375°F for approximately 30 minutes.

Honey Rhubarb Muffins

Reprinted with permission by the
American Beekeeping Federation (ABF)

Ingredients:

Topping:
½ cup sugar
1 teaspoon butter

Muffins:
2½ cups flour
½ teaspoon salt
1 teaspoon baking soda
⅔ cup cooking oil

½ cup honey
½ teaspoon vanilla
½ cup sugar
1 egg
¾ cup buttermilk
1½ cups fresh chopped rhubarb
½ cup chopped nuts

Directions:

Topping:
Combine the sugar and butter, set aside.

Muffins:
Sift flour, salt, and baking soda together and set aside. In a mixing bowl, stir oil, honey, vanilla, sugar and egg until well blended. Alternatively, add the dry ingredients and the buttermilk to the mixture. Stir in rhubarb and nuts. Spoon batter into greased muffin tins. Top with the sugar and butter topping mixture. Bake at 325°F for 35 to 40 minutes.

Soups & Salads

Fruit Soup

Courtesy of Bees-And-Beekeeping.com

Ingredients:

3 pears
3 apples
Juice from ½ lemon
4 cups water
1 tablespoon granulated tapioca
Juice from ½ lemon
⅛ teaspoon cinnamon
3 tablespoons honey

Directions:

Chop the pears and apples. Heat the water until boiling, then add the fruit and cook until tender. Press through a sieve, then add the tapioca and continue cooking until clear. Stir in the lemon juice, cinnamon, and honey. Serve either warm or as a cold fruit soup.

Chilled Strawberry Soup with Mint

Courtesy of American Institute for Cancer Research (AICR)

www.aicr.org

Ingredients:

1 cup unsweetened cold apple juice
2 (16 oz.) bags frozen strawberries, thawed
2-4 tablespoons honey
¼ cup fresh chopped mint
½ cup fat-free vanilla yogurt
4 ginger snaps, crumbled, for garnish (optional)

Directions:

In a blender, puree juice and strawberries with their liquid. With the blender running, drizzle in the honey to taste. Add mint and puree 1 more minute. Strain soup through mesh strainer to remove seeds. Chill, pour into individual bowls, and top with yogurt and crumbled ginger snaps (if desired) before serving.

A Honey of a Chili

Courtesy of the National Honey Board

Ingredients:

1 (15 oz.) package firm tofu
1 tablespoon vegetable oil
1 cup chopped onion
¾ cup chopped green bell pepper
2 cloves garlic, finely chopped
2 tablespoons chili powder
1 teaspoon ground cumin
1 teaspoon salt
½ teaspoon dried oregano
½ teaspoon crushed red pepper flakes
1 (28 oz.) can diced tomatoes, undrained
1 (15½ oz.) can red kidney beans, undrained
1 (8 oz.) can tomato sauce
¼ cup honey
2 tablespoons red wine vinegar

Directions:

Using a cheese grater, shred tofu and freeze in zippered bag or airtight container. Thaw tofu, place in a strainer, and press out excess liquid. In large saucepan or Dutch oven, heat oil over medium-high heat until hot; cook and stir onion, green pepper, and garlic 3 to 5 minutes or until vegetables are tender and begin to brown. Stir in chili powder, cumin, salt, oregano, and crushed red pepper. Stir in tofu; cook and stir 1 minute. Stir in diced tomatoes, kidney beans, tomato sauce, honey, and vinegar. Bring to a boil; reduce heat and simmer, uncovered, 15 to 20 minutes, stirring occasionally.

Sweet and Hot Red Pepper and Tomato Soup

Courtesy of the National Honey Board

Ingredients:

3 tablespoons vegetable oil
2 leeks, white part only, cleaned and chopped
1 stalk celery, chopped
2 medium red bell peppers, seeded and chopped
1 tablespoon grated fresh ginger root
1 (28 oz.) can plum tomatoes, chopped, reserve juice
3 cups chicken or vegetable broth
6 tablespoons honey
2 tablespoons balsamic vinegar
3 tablespoons fresh mint, chopped
3 tablespoons fresh parsley, chopped
Cayenne pepper, to taste
Salt and pepper, to taste

Directions:

In a large saucepan, heat oil over medium heat until hot. Add leeks, celery, and peppers; cook 8 to 10 minutes or until soft. Stir in cayenne and ginger; cook 1 minute. Stir in tomatoes with juice, broth, honey, and vinegar. Bring to a boil; reduce heat and simmer, partially covered, 25 minutes. Remove from heat. Cool soup slightly; puree in blender or food processor until smooth. Season with salt and pepper. Reheat if necessary and serve sprinkled with mint and parsley. Serve warm or cold.

No-Peek Stew

Reprinted with permission by the American Beekeeping
Federation (ABF)

Ingredients:

2 pounds cubed beef
4-5 cubed raw potatoes
6 sliced raw carrots
2 stalks sliced or diced celery
1 onion, chopped
3 teaspoons instant tapioca
1½ teaspoons honey
1 teaspoon salt
¼ teaspoon black pepper
¼ teaspoon garlic salt (optional)
1½ cups tomato juice

Directions:

Put meat in a 9- x 13-inch baking pan. On top of the meat, place
potatoes, carrots, celery, and onion. Mix remainder of ingredients
and pour over all. Seal with foil and bake at 250°F for 5 hours. Do
not peek!

Mango Salad with Grilled Salmon

Fruits & Veggies—More Matters® recipes appear courtesy of Produce for Better Health Foundation (PBH). This recipe meets Centers for Disease Control & Prevention's (CDC) strict nutrition guidelines as a healthy recipe. Find this recipe and others like it online at www.FruitsAndVeggiesMoreMatters.org.

Ingredients:

2 tablespoons rice vinegar
1 tablespoon honey
1 tablespoon grated ginger
¼ cup extra-virgin olive oil
Grilled salmon, to taste
Leafy greens, to taste
Diced mango, to taste
Salt and pepper, to taste

Directions:

Combine the rice vinegar, honey, grated ginger, extra-virgin olive oil, and a dash of salt and pepper in a bowl. Whisk well. Toss with grilled salmon, leafy greens, and diced mango.

Spinach, Red Bell Pepper, and Feta Cheese Salad with Yogurt Dressing

Courtesy of American Institute for Cancer Research (AICR)

www.aicr.org

Ingredients:

½ cup fat-free plain yogurt

1 teaspoon honey

2 tablespoons minced fresh dill

1 (5 oz.) bag baby spinach, coarsely chopped (about 4 cups)

1 large red bell pepper, diced (about 1 cup)

1 stalk celery, trimmed and diced (about 1 cup)

¼ cup thinly sliced green onions (scallions)

1 ounce feta cheese, drained, rinsed and crumbled (about ¼ cup)

Freshly ground black pepper, to taste

Directions:

In a small bowl, stir together yogurt, honey, dill, and black pepper until blended. In a large serving bowl, toss together spinach, red pepper, celery, and green onions. Drizzle dressing over top and lightly toss to coat. Sprinkle with feta and serve.

Fruit and Cheese Salad

Courtesy of American Institute for Cancer Research (AICR)

www.aicr.org

Ingredients:

Dressing:

2 tablespoons raspberry-flavored vinegar

¼ cup fat-free, reduced-sodium chicken broth

2 tablespoons extra-virgin olive oil

1 teaspoon mild-flavored honey

½ teaspoon dried mint leaves

Salad:

6 cups torn, mixed salad greens

1 cup watercress, stems trimmed and chopped

½ cup red onion, very thinly sliced

1 fresh orange, peeled and chopped or 1 (11 oz.) can mandarin orange sections, drained

2 ounces crumbled reduced-fat feta cheese

Directions:

Dressing:

Blend all ingredients at low speed until combined. Transfer to a jar with tight-fitting lid; refrigerate until needed (up to 3 days).

Salad:

In a large bowl, toss mixed greens, watercress, onion, and orange. Shake vinaigrette until thoroughly re-blended, drizzle over salad, and toss lightly. Sprinkle crumbled feta over top and serve.

Papaya, Chicken and Pecan Salad

Courtesy of American Institute for Cancer Research (AICR)

www.aicr.org

Ingredients:

1 cup water
½ pound boneless, skinless chicken breasts
4 cups torn romaine lettuce
1 medium papaya (about 1½ cups), halved, seeded, peeled and cubed
1 cup red pepper strips (about 1 large pepper)
2 scallions, sliced (about ¼ cup)
2 tablespoons red wine vinegar
1 tablespoon fresh lime juice
1 teaspoon honey
1 garlic clove, minced (about ½ teaspoon)
½ teaspoon Dijon mustard
1½ tablespoons olive oil
¼ cup pecan halves, toasted
Salt and freshly ground black pepper, to taste

Directions:

In a 10-inch nonstick skillet, bring the water to boil. Add chicken breasts; return to boil. Cover, reduce heat to low, and cook about 15 minutes or until chicken is cooked through. With a slotted spoon, transfer the chicken to a covered container. Cool in refrigerator.

In a large salad bowl, combine lettuce, papaya, red pepper, and scallions. Whisk together vinegar, lime juice, honey, garlic, and mustard. Slowly add oil in a thin stream. Whisk until well blended. Add salt and pepper, to taste. Cube chicken into bite-sized pieces and combine with the dressing. Toss the chicken and dressing with the salad. Top with pecans.

Spicy Golden Slaw

Courtesy of American Institute for Cancer Research (AICR)

www.aicr.org

Ingredients:

8 cups green cabbage (1 small head, about 1½ pounds), quartered, cored and shredded

1 large green bell pepper, seeded and cut into 2- x ¼-inch strips

1 medium carrot, shredded

½ medium sweet onion, cut in thin crescents

¼ cup white vinegar

3 tablespoons honey

½ teaspoon ground ginger, or to taste

¼ teaspoon ground turmeric

⅛ teaspoon celery seed

1 tablespoon canola oil

Salt and freshly ground black pepper, to taste

Directions:

Place the cabbage, bell pepper, carrot, and onion in a large bowl, tossing until they are evenly combined.

In a small saucepan, combine the vinegar, honey, ginger, turmeric, and celery seed. Over medium heat, bring the mixture to a boil, stirring to dissolve the honey. Remove from heat and mix in the oil. Pour the hot dressing over the vegetables. Toss until they are well combined. Season to taste with salt and pepper and adjust the amount of ginger and celery seed, if desired (a little ginger goes a long way).

Cover the slaw and refrigerate for 4 to 24 hours before serving (it will become more golden after two or three days).

Marinated Edamame Salad

Ingredients:
Dressing:
2 tablespoons olive oil
1 tablespoon honey
2 tablespoons water
¼ cup Dijon mustard
¼ cup lemon juice
2 cloves garlic, minced
¼ cup white wine vinegar
¼ teaspoon basil
¼ teaspoon marjoram
¼ teaspoon rosemary
¼ teaspoon thyme
¼ teaspoon black pepper
¼ teaspoon grated lemon peel

Salad:
2 cups lightly cooked green
beans, cut into bite-sized
pieces with ends trimmed
2 cups cooked and shelled
edamame
¼ cup diced green onion
½ cup chopped red bell pepper
½ cup diced celery
½ cup chopped cucumber
1 cup chopped carrots
2 tablespoons parsley, minced
⅓ cup dried cranberries
2 cups romaine lettuce,
washed

Directions:
Dressing:
Whisk together all ingredients and adjust seasonings to taste.
Set aside.

Salad:
In a salad bowl, toss together all of the salad ingredients, except
the lettuce. Whisk dressing again, pour over salad mixture, and
toss. Cover and refrigerate for at least one hour. When ready to
serve, arrange lettuce on salad plates and top with marinated
salad mixture.

Note: Fresh herbs may be substituted for the dried herbs listed
above. When substituting fresh herbs, use approximately ½ teaspoon of each herb.

Pasta Salad Florentine

Ingredients:
Dressing:
2 tablespoons honey
2½ tablespoons Dijon mustard
3 tablespoons red wine
vinegar
1½ teaspoons dried oregano
½ teaspoon garlic powder

Pasta Salad:
6 ounces small tube-shaped
pasta
2 cups torn fresh spinach
2 cups halved cherry tomatoes
1½ cups frozen peas, placed
in sieve and thawed with hot
running water
½ cup shelled pistachios

Directions:
Dressing:
Combine honey, mustard, vinegar, oregano, and garlic powder.
Mix until well combined.

Pasta Salad:
Drop pasta into boiling water; return to boil. Cook 10 to 15 minutes or until tender. Drain. Toss pasta, spinach, tomatoes, peas, pistachios, and dressing in a large bowl.

Dressings, Dips & Spreads

Smoky Honey Mustard Spread

Courtesy of Janette Marshall from Health Benefits of Honey
www.health-benefits-of-honey.com

Ingredients:

28 ounces (3 ½ cups) plum tomatoes, blended
6 slices smoked bacon, cooked (or 3-4 small smoked sausages)
3-5 garlic cloves
1 small red chili pepper
1 tablespoon mustard
½ pint red wine
½ cup honey (not too sweet)
Chopped oregano, to taste

Directions:

Blend all ingredients together and use as a relish with cold meats or cheese, or as a spread in a sandwich or baguette. There is no cooking involved in this recipe and everything can be blended together in your blender or food processor. This spread is a particularly nice complement to sausage, pork steak, or barbecued chicken.

Honey Mustard Dressing

Courtesy of Janette Marshall from Health Benefits of Honey
www.health-benefits-of-honey.com

Ingredients:

½ cup olive oil
2 teaspoons Dijon mustard
⅛ cup balsamic vinegar
2 teaspoons red wine vinegar
¼ cup grated ginger
Juice and zest of 1 lemon
2 teaspoons coriander
6 small carrots, grated
2 teaspoons honey (preferable raw honey)

Directions:

Mix the olive oil, mustard, balsamic vinegar, red wine vinegar, ginger, lemon juice and zest, and coriander in a saucepan. Gently cook the mixture on low heat, stirring often. Add the grated carrots. The honey mustard sauce will thicken after about 30 minutes. Add the honey at the end (excessive heat will destroy honey's health benefits). Serve this honey mustard dressing with cold or grilled meats. It works well with honey baked ham and white fish dishes.

Balsamic Glaze

Courtesy of American Institute for Cancer Research (AICR)

www.aicr.org

Ingredients:

¼ cup balsamic vinegar

1 tablespoon honey, or to taste

1 teaspoon minced garlic

1 teaspoon minced peeled ginger

1 teaspoon extra-virgin olive oil

1 tomato, seeded and chopped

Salt and freshly ground black pepper, to taste

Directions:

Combine all ingredients in blender and blend just until pureed. Transfer to a non-stick saucepan. Bring mixture to a boil, then immediately reduce heat to medium. Cook, stirring frequently, until sauce is slightly syrupy. Check the taste and if glaze seems too acidic, stir in slightly more honey. Add salt and pepper to taste, if desired.

Drizzle over hot, cooked vegetables and serve immediately or store, covered, in the refrigerator for up to 3 days. Reheat and chill glaze before using.

Cinnamon Flavor Honey Butter

Courtesy of Benefits of Honey, the number one ranked website
on the health benefits of honey
www.benefits-of-honey.com

Ingredients:

¼ cup soft butter or margarine
¼ teaspoon cinnamon powder
½ cup creamed honey
1 tablespoon cream cheese (optional)

Directions:

Blend all ingredients in a bowl and beat well until mixture is
smooth and creamy. Spread the honey butter on piping hot
toasted bread or biscuits. This recipe makes more than enough to
serve 10 people.

Fruit and Nuts Honey Butter

Courtesy of Benefits of Honey, the number one ranked website
on the health benefits of honey
www.benefits-of-honey.com

Ingredients:

¼ cup soft butter or margarine
1 tablespoon peanuts or walnuts
1 tablespoon finely cut dried tropical fruits
½ cup creamed honey

Directions:

Stir and blend all ingredients in a bowl. Mix well. Spread honey
butter on soft bread or biscuits.

Fruit Dip

Courtesy of Benefits of Honey, the number one ranked website
on the health benefits of honey
www.benefits-of-honey.com

Ingredients:

3 cups plain yogurt
1 cup chopped almonds
1 tablespoon honey

Directions:

Combine all ingredients in a bowl and mix well. Chill and serve
with fresh, cut assorted fruits such as strawberries, red and
green apple slices, honey dew melon, and grapes.

Savory Dip

Courtesy of Benefits of Honey, the number one ranked website
on the health benefits of honey
www.benefits-of-honey.com

Ingredients:

½ cup tomato sauce
1 teaspoon cornstarch
½ teaspoon garlic salt
¼ cup honey
2 tablespoons lemon juice

Directions:

Combine all ingredients and cook in a saucepan for a few
minutes. Allow mixture to boil and thicken while stirring it to
smooth the mixture. This serves as a delicious dip for sizzling
hot barbecue wings or chicken nuggets.

Poppy Seed Salad Dressing

Reprinted with permission by the
American Beekeeping Federation (ABF)

Ingredients:

⅓ cup honey
⅓ cup vinegar
1 ¼ cups salad oil
½ teaspoon salt
3 tablespoons Dijon mustard
1 ½ teaspoons poppy seeds

Directions:

Place all ingredients in a blender or mixer bowl. Blend or mix
until oil disappears. Makes 2 cups.

Meat & Poultry Entrées

Easy Fish Sticks with Spinach Basil Dipping Sauce and Spiced Apples

Fruits & Veggies—More Matters® recipes appear courtesy of Produce for Better Health Foundation (PBH). This recipe meets Centers for Disease Control & Prevention's (CDC) strict nutrition guidelines as a healthy recipe. Find this recipe and others like it online at www.FruitsAndVeggiesMoreMatters.org.

Ingredients:

Spinach Basil Dipping Sauce:
1 cup frozen chopped spinach, thawed and drained
½ cup chopped fresh basil
1 clove garlic
¾ cup fat-free plain yogurt
2 tablespoons vinegar
2 teaspoons honey

Fish Sticks:
1 pound frozen pollock (or other white fish, such as haddock or cod), partially thawed
¾ cup whole-wheat bread crumbs

2 tablespoons grated Parmesan cheese
⅛ teaspoon ground black pepper
½ cup flour
2 egg whites, beaten
Nonstick cooking spray

Spiced Apples:
3 Piñata apples
½ cup raisins
¼ cup chopped pecans
½ teaspoon cinnamon
2 teaspoons butter

Directions:

Place rack in center of oven, pre-heat oven to 450°F, and spray baking sheet with cooking spray.

Dipping Sauce:
Place all ingredients in a blender or food processor; blend or process until smooth.

Fish Sticks:
Cut pollock into strips 1-inch wide (easiest when fish is partially, rather than fully, thawed) and place on prepared baking sheet. Mix breading ingredients (bread crumbs, Parmesan cheese, and pepper) in a shallow dish or pie pan; place flour and egg whites in separate dishes. Dip fish sticks in flour, then in egg whites, then in breading mix, coating evenly. Return coated fish sticks to baking sheet, spacing evenly. Bake about 10-12 minutes or until golden brown, turning as needed.

Spiced Apples:
While fish sticks are baking, cut apples in quarters and core them; slice into smaller wedges (about 12 per apple). Toss with raisins, pecans, and cinnamon. Heat butter in medium saucepan. Add fruit mixture. Sauté lightly for about 3-5 minutes. Apples should still be slightly crisp.

Honey Chinese BBQ Pork

Courtesy of Benefits of Honey, the number one
ranked website on the health benefits of honey
www.benefits-of-honey.com

Ingredients:

2 pounds lean pork
2 cloves garlic, blended and ground
½ teaspoon five spices powder
1½ tablespoons soy sauce
½ teaspoon pepper
1 teaspoon salt
1 tablespoon margarine (or vegetable oil)
4-5 tablespoons honey (a rose honey variety works well)

Directions:

Slice pork thinly and tenderize slices. Add seasoning (garlic, five
spices powder, soy sauce, pepper, and salt) and place pork slices
in a container. Leave it in the refrigerator for at least 5 hours
to marinate. Arrange thin pieces of pork on a flat plate to dry.
When dry, cut pork slices into squares of about 4 inches. Barbecue the pork slices with burning charcoal until both sides are
golden in color. Brush the slices with margarine (or vegetable
oil) before grilling and glaze them with honey from time to time.
Serve hot or store in the refrigerator for later use.

Exotic Grilled Honey Wings

Courtesy of Benefits of Honey, the number one
ranked website on the health benefits of honey
www.benefits-of-honey.com

Ingredients:

Marinade:
5 cloves garlic, crushed
5 ginger slices
1 teaspoon five spices powder
1 teaspoon black pepper
2 teaspoons salt
1 tablespoon soy sauce
1 teaspoon dark soy sauce
1 tablespoon honey (such as
macadamia honey)
1 egg

Wings:
8 chicken wings
8 wooden skewers
2 tablespoons honey, for
glazing during grilling

Directions:

Marinade:
Combine all ingredients and set aside.

Wings:
Place wings onto wooden skewers for easy grilling. Marinate
wings in prepared mixture for at least 5 hours. Grill wings in
the oven at 435°F for 15 minutes, then glaze each of them with
honey using a baking brush. Grill for 10 minutes more, turn
over to the other side, and glaze with honey again before grilling
for the final 10 minutes. Serve while hot.

Honey Peking Duck

Courtesy of Benefits of Honey, the number one ranked
website on the health benefits of honey
www.benefits-of-honey.com

Ingredients:

Duck:

1 (5-6 lb.) duck
8 cups water
1 ginger root, sliced
1 scallion, cut into halves
3 tablespoons honey
(any light variety such as
clover, acacia, basswood,
and orange blossom)
1 tablespoon white vinegar

1 tablespoon sherry
1½ tablespoons cornstarch,
dissolved in 3 tablespoons
water

Rolls:

¼ pound scallions, cut into 24
pieces
5 tablespoons hoisin sauce
12 Mandarin crepes
2 cucumbers, peeled and halved

Directions:

Clean and remove the innards of the duck. Wipe duck dry and
store it in a cool, dry place for 4 hours. Fill large wok with
water. Bring to boil. Add ginger, scallion, honey, vinegar, and
sherry. Bring to boil. Pour in dissolved cornstarch. Stir constantly. Place duck in a large strainer above a larger bowl. Scoop
boiling mixture all over the duck for about 10 minutes. Hang
duck again in a cool, dry place for at least 6 hours, until thoroughly dry. Place duck breast side up on a greased rack in an
oven preheated to 350°F. Set a pan filled with 2 inches of water
in the bottom of the oven to collect the drippings. Roast for 30
minutes. Turn duck and roast for 30 minutes more. Turn breast
side up again. Roast for 10 minutes more until skin is crispy.

To slice the duck, use a sharp knife, place it breast side up and
cut downwards towards the head. Slice thinly. Use only the
outer slices, which have skin. Slice both breasts. Slice the legs,
cutting from the joint to the end of the leg. Discard remaining
meat or use it for another dish. Serve meat and skin immediately on a pre-warmed dish. Place all carved meat on a platter,
cover with skin pieces on outside to make the presentation look
like a whole duck. Serves 6.

Honey Glazed Salmon

Courtesy of Janette Marshall from Health Benefits of Honey
www.health-benefits-of-honey.com

Ingredients:

1 fresh salmon fillet per person
2 cloves garlic, crushed
4-6 scallions, chopped
2 tablespoons honey
¼ cup oil
⅛ cup balsamic vinegar
⅛ cup soy sauce
Small dash sesame oil
¼ teaspoon sea salt
1 tablespoon raw brown sugar

Directions:

Blend together all ingredients (except the salmon) to create a marinade. Place the fish fillets into a large, flat oven-proof glass dish. Make sure to oil the dish first to prevent the salmon from sticking while cooking. Pour the marinade over the fillets, cover with plastic wrap, and leave in the refrigerator overnight. This allows the fish to absorb all those wonderful flavors.

Set oven to medium heat. Remove marinated fish from the refrigerator and remove the plastic wrap from the dish. Tip the dish slightly and spoon the marinade over the salmon so that it is equally covered. Place in the oven for approximately 20 minutes. Check to see if the salmon is cooked by pulling at the flesh with a fork. It is cooked once it appears to be flaking. Remove from the oven and set aside.

In a saucepan, slowly heat (not boil) a little more balsamic vinegar and another spoonful of honey. Place the cooked fish onto pre-heated plates or a serving dish and pour the excess marinade into the saucepan. Stir this extra sauce together and pour over salmon. Decorate with a few herb leaves and thin slices of either lemon, lime, or orange or a rich tomato salsa.

Honey-Mustard Salmon

Ingredients:

4 tablespoons honey
3 tablespoons mustard (Dijon works well)
2 teaspoons lemon juice
4 (6 oz.) salmon steaks
Pepper, to taste

Directions:

Preheat oven to 350°F. Mix the honey, mustard, and lemon juice in a small dish. Coat the salmon steaks with the mixture. Season with pepper. Wrap the salmon steaks and the extra sauce in foil and place them in a medium baking dish. Bake for approximately 25 to 30 minutes, or until the fish flakes easily when poked with a fork. Drizzle a little of the remaining sauce over the salmon steaks and serve hot with a side of rice.

Honey Walnut Shrimp

Courtesy of Janette Marshall from Health Benefits of Honey
www.health-benefits-of-honey.com

Ingredients:

1 tablespoon butter
1 cup whole shelled walnuts
3 tablespoons sugar
3 tablespoons mayonnaise
1 tablespoon honey
2 tablespoons sweetened condensed milk
½ teaspoon lemon juice
1 cup flour
½ teaspoon salt
1 cup water
2-3 cups good-quality cooking oil, for the wok
1 pound shrimp, shelled and cleaned

Directions:

Heat the butter in a pan over medium heat until melted. Add the walnuts and stir constantly for one minute. Add 2 tablespoons sugar and continue stirring all these ingredients together for 2 minutes.

Sauce:

Mix together the mayonnaise, honey, sweetened condensed milk, and lemon juice. Set the sauce aside.

Shrimp Batter:

Mix together the flour, remaining teaspoon of sugar, salt, and water. Stir these ingredients until smooth.

Shrimp:

Heat 2 to 3 cups of cooking oil in a wok. Add shrimp to the batter and, using a fork to pick them out, shake any excess batter off and place into the hot oil. (It is recommended to use 8 to 10 shrimp at a time to avoid overloading the wok.) Cook the shrimp until they become a light golden brown color. Repeat and when each batch is ready, place them on paper towels to soak up the excess oil. Once the shrimp are all cooked, stir them into your sauce and serve.

Honey Sweet and Sour Meatballs

Reprinted with permission by the American Beekeeping
Federation (ABF)

Ingredients:

1- 1½ pounds ground beef
1½ teaspoons seasoning salt
¼ cup milk
½ teaspoon pepper
½ cup butter
½ cup honey
¼ cup wine vinegar
1 medium-sized onion, cut into
1-inch sections
2 tablespoons soy sauce

1 (8 oz.) can pineapple slices
with juice
¼ teaspoon cayenne pepper, or
to taste
2 tablespoons cornstarch
2 ounces water

Directions:

Combine beef with seasoning salt, milk, and pepper and mix
thoroughly. Shape into meatballs and fry in oil or butter until browned well and completely cooked. In a large sauce pan,
combine honey, vinegar, onion, soy sauce, and pineapple juice
(set pineapple slices aside) and bring to a boil. Add cayenne and
reduce to medium heat for three to five minutes. In a cup, combine cornstarch and water and mix until no lumps remain, then
add to sauce to thicken. Place meatballs and pineapple slices in
a serving dish and cover with sweet and sour sauce. Recipe can
be doubled or tripled to serve more.

Ham and Sweet Potato Shish Kabobs

Reprinted with permission by the American Beekeeping
Federation (ABF)

Ingredients:

1 large sweet potato, peeled
1 (8 oz.) can unsweetened pineapple chunks
¼ cup butter
3 teaspoons brown sugar
2 large apples, cut into 1-inch pieces
1 zucchini or yellow squash, cut into ¼-inch slices
1 pound ham, cut into 1-inch squares
2 teaspoons honey

Directions:

Put sweet potato into a saucepan with enough water to cover
and boil for 10 minutes or until almost tender. Drain, cool, and
cut into 1-inch squares. Drain pineapple, reserving the juice.
In a mixing bowl combine butter, brown sugar and juice from
pineapple, mixing thoroughly. Add pineapple chunks, apples,
squash, ham, and sweet potato and keep in the refrigerator for
2 to 3 hours or overnight. Drain marinade mixture and thread
on skewers for grilling. Grill for 15 minutes, turning every 5
minutes and baste with honey with each turn.

Scallops and Sweet Taters

Reprinted with permission by the American Beekeeping
Federation (ABF)

Ingredients:

3-4 teaspoons olive oil
1 medium-sized onion, sliced in
1-inch squares
1 teaspoon minced garlic
6 medium-sized mushrooms,
thinly sliced
1 red bell pepper, sliced
in 1-inch pieces
1 medium-sized zucchini squash
1 medium-sized yellow squash,
sliced thin
2 teaspoons salt

1½-2 pounds scallops
½ cup honey
4 tablespoons butter
4 teaspoons flour
1½ cups chicken stock
1 cup light cream or half-and-half
1 egg yolk
3-4 medium sweet potatoes
¼ cup pecan pieces
4-5 cups prepared rice or
noodles

Directions:

Scallops:

Heat a large skillet or wok to a good heat and add olive oil. After 20
to 30 seconds, add sliced onions, garlic, sliced mushrooms, red pepper,
and squash. Stir frequently and add one teaspoon of salt. Cook for 3
minutes, stirring frequently, then add scallops and ¼ cup of honey to
mixture. Cook for another three minutes, stirring frequently. When scallops are just lightly cooked, cover and set aside to prepare the sauce.

To make the velouté sauce, mix the butter and flour together in a medium saucepan and, once well mixed, add all of the stock and half of the
cream (or half-and-half). Cook over low heat until thickened, whisking
often. To finish the velouté sauce, blend the egg yolk and remaining half
of the cream. This is called a liaison. Add ¼ cup of the hot velouté sauce
to the egg and cream mixture to warm the egg. After a quick whisk,
return to the velouté. Bring the mixture to a boil while whisking and
remove from the heat, continuing the whisk for another 30 seconds or
so. Add the velouté to your cooked scallops and vegetables and cover.

Sweet Potatoes:

To prepare the sweet potatoes, slice into French fries and deep-fry until
tender. Remove, drain, pat dry, and place on a plate. Drizzle with some
of the remaining honey and sprinkle with pecan pieces and a dash of
salt. Add one cup of rice (or noodles) to plate and cover generously with
scallops and vegetables. Makes 4 servings.

Honey Chicken

Courtesy of Janette Marshall from Health Benefits of Honey
www.health-benefits-of-honey.com

Ingredients:

8 chicken drumsticks or thighs
¼ cup mustard
1 cup button mushrooms, chopped or sliced
¼ cup honey
Salt, black pepper and oregano, to taste

Directions:

Prepare the chicken by washing and patting dry. Mix all the other ingredients together in a bowl and dip your chicken to coat with the tasty sauce mixture. Lay each piece of chicken in a large roasting pan, leaving a little room between each one. Bake at 375°F for approximately 30 minutes; Turn chicken pieces halfway through cooking and use a pastry brush to coat them with the remainder of the sauce.

Honey Bourbon Chicken

Courtesy of Janette Marshall from Health Benefits of Honey
www.health-benefits-of-honey.com

Ingredients:

4 boneless chicken breasts
1 cup flour
2 red onions, chopped
2 cloves garlic
2 stalks celery
½ pint chicken stock
2 teaspoons mustard
2 teaspoons Worcestershire sauce
1 tablespoon honey
1 tablespoon bourbon
Salt and pepper, to taste

Directions:

Dice and flour the washed and dried chicken pieces. Set them aside. Chop the red onions, garlic cloves, and celery. Fry these gently together until soft. In a large pan, add chicken stock, mustard, Worcestershire sauce, honey, and bourbon. Salt and pepper to taste. Stir all ingredients together, add the chicken pieces, and place in a casserole dish. Cook in the center of a 400°F oven for approximately an hour.

Cajun Style Honey Barbecue Chicken

Courtesy of Janette Marshall from Health Benefits of Honey
www.health-benefits-of-honey.com

Ingredients:

8 chicken pieces (breasts or thighs are best)
4-6 cobs of corn, cut into chunks
2 teaspoons chopped garlic
2 teaspoons freshly ground black pepper

2 teaspoons paprika
1-2 teaspoons cayenne pepper
1 teaspoon ground cumin powder
3 tablespoons melted butter
3 tablespoons honey

Directions:

Combine all the ingredients in a deep bowl and toss until coated well. Leave in the refrigerator overnight to allow the ingredients to soak into the chicken and corn. Cook over a medium heat grill.

Vegetarian Entrées

Vegetables with Spicy Honey Peanut Sauce

Courtesy of the National Honey Board

Ingredients:

½ cup honey
¼ cup peanut butter
2 tablespoons soy sauce
1 tablespoon chopped fresh cilantro
⅛ teaspoon crushed red pepper flakes
4 cups broccoli florets
4 cups sliced carrots
4 cups snow peas
6 cups cooked white rice

Directions:

Combine honey, peanut butter, soy sauce, cilantro, and red pepper in small bowl; mix well and set aside. Steam vegetables until crisp-tender; drain well. Toss steamed vegetables with peanut sauce in large bowl. Serve immediately over rice.

Thai Noodles with Tofu and Snow Peas

Courtesy of the National Honey Board

Ingredients:

1 (15 oz.) package extra firm
tofu, drained, pressed,
and cut into ½-inch pieces
1 (9 oz.) package fresh Asian-
style noodles
4 ounces snow peas, trimmed
and diagonally cut
¼ cup chopped fresh cilantro

Marinade:
⅓ cup rice vinegar
¼ cup honey
2 tablespoons peanut butter
2 tablespoons soy sauce
2 tablespoons vegetable oil
1 tablespoon sesame oil
2 cloves garlic, finely chopped
½ teaspoon crushed red pepper
¼ teaspoon ground ginger

Directions:

In a medium bowl, combine marinade ingredients. Add tofu;
marinate 30 minutes. Cook noodles and snow peas in 3 quarts
boiling water 1 to 2 minutes, or until peas are crisp-tender;
drain. Rinse with cold water; drain. Place in a large bowl; add
tofu and marinade. Toss gently to coat. Add cilantro; toss to
coat.

Stuffed Sweet Peppers

Courtesy of the National Honey Board

Ingredients:

1 tablespoon vegetable or olive oil
¾ cup uncooked long-grain rice
4 green onions, thinly sliced
¼ cup finely chopped fresh parsley
¼ teaspoon ground cinnamon
¼ teaspoon black pepper
¼ teaspoon salt
1 (14½ oz.) can vegetable broth
4 medium green bell peppers, cut lengthwise in half, seeded
1 (28 oz.) can crushed tomatoes in puree
¼ cup honey
½ teaspoon crushed red pepper flakes
1 (8 ¾ oz.) can garbanzo beans, drained
⅓ cup dried currants or raisins

Directions:

In large saucepan, heat oil over medium-high heat until hot; cook and stir rice, onion, and parsley 3 to 5 minutes or until rice begins to brown. Stir in cinnamon, pepper, and salt. Gradually add vegetable broth. Bring to a boil, reduce heat, cover, and simmer for 18 to 20 minutes or until liquid is absorbed and rice is cooked through. Meanwhile, cook green pepper halves in boiling water 5 to 7 minutes or until peppers are crisp-tender; drain. Combine tomatoes, honey, and crushed red pepper in 13- x 9-inch baking pan; mix well. Remove ¼ cup sauce; set aside. Arrange pepper halves on sauce in baking pan. When rice is cooked, remove from heat; stir in garbanzo beans, dried currants, and reserved ¼ cup sauce. Divide rice evenly among pepper halves in baking pan. Cover pan tightly with foil. Bake at 350°F for 30 minutes.

Spicy Grilled Tofu

Courtesy of the National Honey Board

Ingredients:

1 (14 oz.) package extra firm tofu, drained and cut lengthwise
into 8 slices
½ cup fresh lime juice
⅓ cup honey
¼ cup soy sauce
2 teaspoons chili paste with garlic
3 cloves garlic, minced (about 1 tablespoon)
¼ teaspoon ground black pepper

Directions:

Place tofu slices on several layers of paper towels; cover with
additional paper towels. Let stand 20 minutes, pressing down
occasionally with your hands to squeeze out water. Arrange tofu
in single layer in 13- x 9-inch glass baking dish. Whisk together
lime juice, honey, soy sauce, chili paste, garlic, and pepper in
small bowl. Pour over tofu, coating each slice. Cover tightly with
plastic wrap and chill 4 hours or overnight. Spray grill rack
or pan with non-stick cooking spray. Heat grill or grill pan to
medium heat. Remove tofu slices from baking dish, reserving
marinade. Grill tofu slices 3 to 4 minutes on each side or until
browned and crisp on the outside. Return tofu to baking dish
and toss with reserved marinade. Serve immediately.

Southwestern Lasagna
Courtesy of the National Honey Board

Ingredients:
1 tablespoon vegetable oil
1 medium onion, thinly sliced
1 clove garlic, finely chopped
1 tablespoon chili powder
1 tablespoon paprika
¾ cup water
1 (6 oz.) can tomato paste
¼ cup honey
¼ cup fresh lime juice
1 (15 oz.) can black beans, undrained
1 (12 oz.) can vacuum-packed whole kernel corn
6 medium corn tortillas, cut in quarters
1 (15 oz.) package part skim ricotta cheese
1 (7 oz.) can whole green chiles, cut lengthwise into ½-inch strips
½ cup (2 oz.) shredded Monterey Jack cheese

Directions:
In a medium saucepan, heat oil over medium-high heat until hot; cook and stir onions and garlic 3 to 5 minutes or until onion is tender. Add chili powder and paprika; cook and stir 1 minute. Stir in water, tomato paste, honey, and lime juice until well mixed. Stir in black beans and corn. Bring to a boil; reduce heat and simmer 5 minutes. Spoon ⅓ of sauce into 1½-quart rectangular baking pan; arrange ½ of tortilla quarters evenly over sauce in pan. Spread with ½ of ricotta cheese and arrange ½ of green chile strips evenly over cheese. Repeat with ⅓ of sauce, remaining tortillas, ricotta cheese, and green chilies. Spread remaining sauce evenly over top of lasagna; sprinkle evenly with shredded cheese. Bake at 350°F for 20 to 25 minutes or until heated.

Grilled Tofu Kabobs with Chipotle Marinade

Courtesy of the National Honey Board

Ingredients:

Chipotle Marinade:
1 cup vegetable broth
1 clove garlic, minced
⅓ cup honey
¼ cup tamari soy sauce
1 chipotle in adobo, minced
1½ tablespoons adobo sauce
1½ teaspoons granulated onion powder
1 tablespoon Dijon mustard
1 tablespoon fresh chopped cilantro

Grilled Tofu Kabobs:
2 (14 oz.) packages extra firm tofu
2 cups Chipotle Marinade
3 medium zucchini, cut into 1-inch circles
1 medium red bell pepper, cut into 1-inch chunks
1 medium red onion, cut into 1-inch wedges
12 cherry tomatoes
1 cup pineapple cubes

Directions:

Marinade:
Whisk together broth, garlic, honey, soy sauce, chipotle, and adobo sauce in 2-cup liquid measuring cup. Add onion powder, mustard, and cilantro; mix well.

Kabobs:
Slice each block of tofu in half horizontally and, in a cross-hatch pattern, make two slices vertically and two slices horizontally for a total of 36 tofu cubes. Place tofu in a 9- x 13-inch baking dish. Pour marinade over tofu, cover, and refrigerate for 1 to 24 hours. Set and light fire using coals or mesquite about 30 minutes before cooking time. Soak bamboo skewers in hot water for 20 minutes. Alternating ingredients, thread tofu, vegetables, and pineapple cubes on skewers. Place kabobs over hot coals on well-oiled grill rack. Cook about 10 minutes, or until done, turning once and taking care that vegetables don't burn.

Garden Stir-Fry
Courtesy of the National Honey Board

Ingredients:
1 tablespoon vegetable oil
1 clove garlic, minced
1 small onion, vertically sliced
3 medium zucchini, julienned
1 medium yellow squash, julienned
1 large carrot, julienned
¼ cup honey
2 tablespoons lemon juice
1 teaspoon salt
1 teaspoon pepper

Directions:
Heat oil in a heavy skillet or stir-fry pan over high heat. Add garlic and onion and cook until fragrant, 1-2 minutes. Add all remaining ingredients and stir-fry until vegetables are crisp-tender.

Honey-Roasted Parsnips with Sweet Potatoes and Apples

Courtesy of American Institute for Cancer Research (AICR)
www.aicr.org

Ingredients:

1½ cups parsnips, peeled and cut into bite-sized chunks
1 large sweet potato, peeled and cut into bite-sized chunks
2 firm Gala or Fuji apples, peeled, cored and cut into bite-sized chunks
1 tablespoon canola oil
1 tablespoon honey
2 tablespoons balsamic vinegar, or to taste
Nonstick cooking spray
Salt and freshly ground black pepper, to taste

Directions:

Preheat oven to 375°F. Coat a casserole dish with nonstick cooking spray and set aside. In a large mixing bowl, place the parsnips, sweet potato, and apples and set aside. In a microwave-safe bowl, mix together the canola oil and honey. Place in a microwave and warm for 10 seconds. Mix in balsamic vinegar. Pour onto vegetables and apples. Toss to coat well. Transfer to casserole dish, cover, and bake until tender, about 1 hour.

Caramelized Carrots and Orange Squash

Courtesy of American Institute for Cancer Research (AICR)

www.aicr.org

Ingredients:

½ cup raisins

⅔ cup apple juice

2 pounds carrots, peeled and sliced diagonally, ¼-inch pieces

1 small butternut squash, peeled and cubed, ½-inch cubes

1 small acorn squash (about 1 pound), seeds removed, peeled, cubed, ½-inch cubes

3 tablespoons light olive oil

2½ tablespoons dark honey

½ teaspoon ground cinnamon

½ cup apricot halves, cut into small pieces

Sea salt and coarsely ground black pepper, to taste

Directions:

Preheat oven to 400°F. Soak the raisins in apple juice. Line a large baking sheet with two sheets of parchment paper. In large bowl, mix carrots, butternut squash, acorn squash, oil, honey, cinnamon, and salt and pepper to taste. Spread the mixture on baking pan. Bake until carrots (which take the longest to bake) are just soft and then add the raisins and apricots. Bake about 10 minutes longer, until carrots are soft enough for fork to prick through. Serve immediately or, if refrigerating for several hours or more, pour ⅓ cup apple juice over vegetables to keep moist before reheating.

Poached Figs with Honey and Red Wine Sauce

Ingredients:

1 cup dry red wine
2 tablespoons flour
¼ cup honey
2 sticks cinnamon
7-8 fresh figs

Directions:

Pour the wine into a pan and add the flour. Allow the flour to dissolve and then warm the mixture over medium heat. In a separate saucepan, warm the honey until it reaches a syrupy consistency. Add the warmed honey and cinnamon sticks to the wine mixture. Heat the mixture on medium-low for another 7 to 8 minutes. Turn the burner down to low and add the figs, standing them up straight in the pan. Place a lid on the pan and allow to cook until figs are fully cooked, stirring occasionally. The figs should take approximately 20 minutes to cook.

Before serving, remove the cinnamon sticks from the pan. Neatly place the figs in individual bowls and drizzle the honey and red wine sauce over the top. Serve while hot.

Side Dishes
& Snacks

Honey Candied Sweet Potatoes
Courtesy of Bees-And-Beekeeping.com

Ingredients:
¾ cup honey
2 tablespoons shortening
¼ teaspoon mace
¼ teaspoon cinnamon
6 sweet potatoes, boiled and peeled

Directions:
Mix the honey, shortening, mace, and cinnamon in a large frying pan. Bring to a boil and cook until the mixture thickens. Place the sweet potatoes and 4 tablespoons of water into the honey syrup and turn potatoes frequently, coating well with the syrup. Cook the potatoes under low heat for 20 minutes.

Green Bean Vinaigrette

Courtesy of American Institute for Cancer Research (AICR)

www.aicr.org

Ingredients:

1 (1 lb.) bag frozen green beans, thawed (or 3 cups fresh green beans)
1 (14 oz.) jar pimentos, drained
1 tablespoon minced chives
1 tablespoon olive oil
½ tablespoon balsamic vinegar, or to taste
½ teaspoon Dijon mustard
½ teaspoon honey
1 clove garlic, minced
Salt and pepper, to taste

Directions:

In a medium bowl, mix together green beans, pimentos, and chives. In a separate small bowl, whisk together oil, vinegar, mustard, honey, and garlic, then toss into green beans. Season with salt and pepper before serving.

Carrots and Dried Apricots with Cinnamon

Courtesy of American Institute for Cancer Research (AICR)

www.aicr.org

Ingredients:

2 cups baby carrots
2 teaspoons canola oil
½ cup orange juice
8 whole dried apricots, cut into thin strips
¼ teaspoon ground ginger
⅛ teaspoon ground cinnamon
1 teaspoon honey
Salt and freshly ground black pepper, to taste

Directions:

Halve the carrots lengthwise, leaving the thinnest ones whole. Heat the canola oil in a medium skillet over medium-high heat. Add the carrots, stirring until they are coated with the oil. Pour in the orange juice. Add the apricots, ginger, and cinnamon. When the liquid boils, reduce the heat and simmer, stirring occasionally, until the carrots are tender and the juice is syrupy and puddles around the carrots, 8 to 10 minutes. Season the carrots to taste with salt and pepper.

Remove from the heat and mix in the honey. Serve the carrots warm or at room temperature.

Perfect Honey Pizza

Courtesy of Benefits of Honey, the number one ranked
website on the health benefits of honey
www.benefits-of-honey.com

Ingredients:

1-2 tablespoons honey (try Fireweed, Rewarewa or Tawari
varieties)
5 slices soft white bread
3 tomatoes, finely chopped and drained
1 cup ham slices (cut into small 1- x 1-inch squares)
10 tablespoons shredded mozzarella cheese
Sesame, oregano, basil, pepper, thyme, and rosemary, to taste

Directions:

Spread honey on bread slices. Lay tomatoes pieces evenly on the
bread, followed by ham squares. Spread cheese on top and finish
off by sprinkling the mixed spices. Place in the oven at 285°F
for 25-30 minutes.

Oriental Honey Pickles

Courtesy of Benefits of Honey, the number one ranked
website on the health benefits of honey
www.benefits-of-honey.com

Ingredients:

Pickling Syrup:

6-7 tablespoons lemon juice
(substitute 4-5 tablespoons
white vinegar for stronger
pickles, or use a mixture of
lemon juice and vinegar if you
prefer)

2 tablespoons honey (a light,
mild floral variety)

4 tablespoons water

2 teaspoons sea salt

Pickles:

1 small carrot

½ small turnip

½ cucumber

2 slices Chinese cabbage

½ slice pineapple (not too
ripe)

1-2 long red chili peppers

1 tablespoon roasted sesame
seeds

1 tablespoon ground roasted
peanuts (optional)

Directions:

Pickling Syrup:

Mix together the lemon juice, honey, water, and sea salt in a
bowl and set aside.

Pickles:

Wash all vegetables. Remove seeds from cucumber and chili
peppers. Cut carrot, turnip, cucumber, cabbage, and chili peppers into thin strips about 2 inches long. Cut the pineapple into
small, thin sections. Mix the pickling syrup, sesame seeds, and
peanuts (optional) into the vegetables and pack them into a
glass jar. Enjoy immediately or store in refrigerator for stron-
ger-tasting pickles.

Note: It is difficult to specify the amount of vegetables needed
due to the odd sizes they may come in. Therefore, you may
have to do some adjustments in terms of the amount of pickling
syrup that you prepare.

Sweet and Salty Crunchy Mix

Courtesy of American Institute for Cancer Research (AICR)

www.aicr.org

Ingredients:

2 cups cereal, preferably whole-grain (such as old-fashioned rolled oats, puffed whole-wheat or brown rice, or low-fat granola)

2 cups thin pretzels, broken into small pieces

½ cup walnuts or almonds

½ cup pumpkin seeds

½ teaspoon turmeric

2 cups mixed dried fruit, preferably unsweetened (such as raisins, berries, apples, or dates)

¼-⅓ cup honey

Nonstick cooking spray

Directions:

Preheat oven to 350°F if baking 15 to 20 minutes, and 300°F for slower baking, which will take 45 to 60 minutes. (Slow baking takes more time but deepens the flavor.) Lightly coat bottom of two baking sheets with nonstick cooking spray and set aside.

In a large bowl, mix together the cereal, pretzels, nuts, and seeds until well combined. Stir in the turmeric until evenly distributed. Stir in the dried fruit. In a heat-resistant measuring cup, gently warm the honey in a microwave to thin its consistency, or on the stovetop using a small saucepan containing hot water. Slowly add just enough of the honey into the cereal mixture, stirring constantly, until the mixture begins to adhere and form clusters. Spread the mixture on the baking sheets in a thin layer. Spray with nonstick cooking spray. Bake until cereal is lightly browned, stirring once if baking at 350°F or 3-4 times if slow baking at 300°F.

Remove from oven and cool on a rack. Serve immediately or store in a sealed container or zip-lock plastic bags.

Honey Whole-Wheat Bread

Courtesy of Janette Marshall from Health Benefits of Honey

www.health-benefits-of-honey.com

Ingredients:

7 cups whole-wheat flour (or 3 cups whole-wheat and 4 cups all-purpose flour)

2 packets quick-rise yeast

½ teaspoon salt

1⅔ cups very hot water (120°F-130°F)

½ cup honey

¼ cup vegetable oil

1 large egg

Poppy seeds, pumpkin seeds, crushed almonds or mixed nuts, to taste (optional)

Directions:

Preheat the oven to 350°F. In a large bowl, add together 3 cups of whole-wheat flour, yeast, and salt. Add hot water. Beat together the honey, oil, and egg and add this to your mixture along with one more cup of flour. Add the remaining flour slowly until the bread mixture no longer feels sticky. Punch and knead the dough for at least 10 minutes. Spread it out on a lightly floured surface, fold it, and push and punch it out again. The dough should feel smooth and elastic when you pull it. Cut the dough mixture into two equal halves, cover with plastic wrap, and let it sit for ten minutes.

Take the two halves of dough and shape them into loaf shapes. Place them on a cookie sheet or flat baking tray, cover with a clean tea towel or more plastic wrap, and place in a warm room. Wait until the dough doubles in size (about 30 minutes). Use a sharp knife to cut an 'x' shape on top of each loaf and place them in the middle of the preheated oven.

Once the bread is golden brown (approximately 20 minutes) place aluminum foil over the loaves and bake for another 10 minutes. The bread is done when a sharp knife is inserted and comes out clean. Take the bread out of the oven and, using a pastry brush, spread either honey or melted butter over the top to make it shine. Sprinkle any optional extras on top at this time.

Place the loaves on a cooling rack and wait until they are still slightly warm before cutting.

Honey Cole Slaw

Reprinted with permission by the American Beekeeping
Federation (ABF)

Ingredients:

½ cup mayonnaise
2 tablespoons honey
¼ teaspoon onion powder
4 cups grated cabbage or 1 package prepared slaw
2 tablespoons vinegar
½ teaspoon salt
¼ teaspoon celery seed

Directions:

Combine all ingredients (except cabbage). Pour over shredded
cabbage and mix well.

Cinnamon Raisin Granola

Reprinted with permission by the American Beekeeping
Federation (ABF)

Ingredients:

4 cups old-fashioned oats
1 cup shredded coconut
¼ cup packed brown sugar
¼ cup vegetable oil
¼ cup honey
1 teaspoon ground cinnamon
1½ teaspoons vanilla extract
1 cup raisins

Directions:

In a large bowl, combine oats and coconut, set aside. In a sauce-pan, combine brown sugar, oil, honey, and cinnamon, then bring to a boil. Remove from heat and stir in vanilla extract. Pour over oat mixture, stirring to coat thoroughly. Spread in a large shallow baking pan and bake at 350°F for 15-20 minutes, stirring occasionally. Cool and add raisins. Store in an airtight container.

Beverages

Fruity Iced Tea

Courtesy of American Institute for Cancer Research (AICR)
www.aicr.org

Ingredients:

6 cups water
1 cinnamon stick
1 teaspoon whole cloves
6 black tea bags
3-4 cups apricot or peach nectar
Honey, to taste

Directions:

In large saucepan, simmer water, cinnamon stick, and cloves
for 15 minutes, covered. Turn off heat. Add tea bags. Steep 2-5
minutes, depending on the strength you prefer. Remove tea bags.
Add apricot nectar. Add honey, to taste. Strain to remove spices.
Refrigerate until cold.

Green Tea Slush with Apricot Nectar

Courtesy of American Institute for Cancer Research (AICR)

www.aicr.org

Ingredients:

3 cups prepared green tea (use decaffeinated if desired)

1 cup apricot nectar

1 cup crushed ice

1 tablespoon honey

Directions:

In blender or food processor, combine all ingredients and puree until smooth.

Peanut Butter and Banana Smoothie

Courtesy of American Institute for Cancer Research (AICR)

www.aicr.org

Ingredients:

4 cups fat-free milk
4 tablespoons smooth peanut butter
4 frozen bananas
⅛-¼ teaspoon cinnamon
¼ teaspoon vanilla
Honey, to taste

Directions:

In blender, place milk and peanut butter. Blend for 30 seconds. Add bananas, cinnamon, vanilla, and honey. Blend until mixture is completely combined. Serve immediately.

Minted Honeydew Cooler

Courtesy of American Institute for Cancer Research (AICR)

www.aicr.org

Ingredients:

3 cups cubed honeydew melon

1 cup unsweetened pineapple juice

1 cup crushed ice

2 tablespoons honey

2 tablespoons fresh mint leaves

Directions:

Combine all ingredients in blender or food processor and puree until smooth.

Kiddy Fruity Honey Smoothie

Courtesy of Benefits of Honey, the number one ranked
website on the health benefits of honey
www.benefits-of-honey.com

Ingredients:

½ banana
5 strawberries
1 cup plain yogurt
2 teaspoons honey
Ice cubes

Directions:

Cut up the banana into pieces and put them into a blender with
the strawberries. Add yogurt, honey, and ice cubes. Blend the
mixture to make a delicious, smooth, cool drink.

Orange Delight Juice

Fruits & Veggies—More Matters® recipes appear courtesy of Produce for Better Health Foundation (PBH). This recipe meets Centers for Disease Control & Prevention's (CDC) strict nutrition guidelines as a healthy recipe. Find this recipe and others like it online at www. FruitsAndVeggiesMoreMatters.org.

Ingredients:

1 cup 100% orange juice
2 bananas
1 cup 100% apple juice
1 teaspoon honey
⅛ teaspoon cinnamon
1 cup crushed ice

Directions:

Blend all ingredients in a blender on high speed until frothy. Serve.

Honey Punch

Reprinted with permission by the American Beekeeping
Federation (ABF)

Ingredients:

1 cup honey
½ cup hot water
½ cup lemon juice
1½ cups orange juice
1 (46 oz.) can unsweetened pineapple juice
1½ cups cold water
1-2 liters ginger ale
Lemon or orange slices and maraschino cherries, for garnish

Directions:

Add honey to hot water; add fruit juices and cold water. Chill.
Just before serving, add ginger ale. Garnish with lemon or orange slices and maraschino cherries.

Desserts

Honey Popcorn Balls

Courtesy of Bees-And-Beekeeping.com

Ingredients:

1 cup honey
1 large bowl popped popcorn

Directions:

Boil the honey, stirring constantly, until it forms a soft ball
when a drop is placed in cold water. Drizzle the honey over
the popcorn. Mix the popcorn and honey thoroughly. Form into
balls, and place on waxed paper. Allow the honey popcorn balls
to cool before serving.

No-Bake Fruit Cake

Courtesy of Bees-And-Beekeeping.com

Ingredients:

2 cups rolled oats

1¾ cups whole-wheat flour

2 cups grape juice (or any type of fruit juice you prefer)

2 pounds raisins

2 pounds currants

2 pounds dates

2 pounds English walnuts

¼ pound candied lemon peel

¼ pound orange peel

⅓ pound citron

1 cup honey

6 tablespoons olive oil

1 teaspoon cinnamon

1 teaspoon cloves

1 teaspoon allspice

1 teaspoon nutmeg

Directions:

Combine the oats and wheat flour in a bowl and pour the fruit juice over. Let mixture sit overnight. Finely chop all of the fruit, fruit peels, and nuts, then mix them all together. Combine all of the ingredients together and mix thoroughly. Line with waxed paper whatever type of pans you wish to use and pour the mixture into the pans. Place a heavy weight on top of the mixture in the pans and allow to sit for 24 hours, after which the fruit cake will be ready to serve. This recipe makes 11 pounds of fruit cake.

French Nougat

Courtesy of Bees-And-Beekeeping.com

Ingredients:

1 quart honey
1 pound sugar
12 egg whites
3 pounds blanched almonds
Vanilla extract, to taste

Directions:

Combine the honey and sugar in a saucepan. Whisk the egg whites and have the almonds ready to use. Heat the honey-sugar mixture over low heat, stirring until the sugar is completely dissolved. Slowly blend in the egg whites and continue stirring until the mixture does not stick to your fingers (don't burn yourself doing this test, especially while the mixture is still sticky). Stir in the almonds and vanilla, and then spread the candy out in a layer ½-inch deep on waxed paper. Cut into bite-sized pieces once the candy has cooled.

Honey Taffy

Courtesy of Bees-And-Beekeeping.com

Ingredients:

2 cups sugar
¾ cup honey
1 cup water
2 tablespoons butter

Directions:

Combine the sugar, honey, and water in a saucepan and cook until it reaches 278°F or until the soft-crack stage. (The soft-crack stage is when a bit of the syrup is dropped into cold water and it forms solid threads that are flexible, not brittle. The threads can be bent slightly without breaking.) While heating the mixture, stir constantly until the sugar is dissolved, and then stir occasionally to prevent scorching. Remove from heat and stir in the butter. Stir as little as possible, only enough to mix in the butter. Pour the candy into greased pans and allow to cool until it is safe to handle with bare hands. Gather the taffy into a ball and pull it repeatedly until it becomes somewhat firm and light in color. Stretch the taffy out into a long rope and cut into bite-sized pieces with a pair of scissors. Wrap each piece of taffy in waxed paper.

Honey Apple Pudding

Courtesy of Bees-And-Beekeeping.com

Ingredients:

2 cups stewed apples
1 cup honey
½ cup brown sugar
4 tablespoons shortening
2 cups fine bread crumbs
1½ cups flour
2 tablespoons baking powder
2 teaspoons cinnamon
½ teaspoon cloves

Directions:

Combine all ingredients and beat until thoroughly mixed. Pour into a baking dish and bake for 35 minutes at 300°F. Serve the pudding with a thin applesauce that has been sweetened with honey.

Avocado Delight

Courtesy of Benefits of Honey, the number one ranked
website on the health benefits of honey
www.benefits-of-honey.com

Ingredients:

3 large, fully ripe avocados
1 tablespoon honey, or to taste
½ cup low-fat cream
½ cup milk
1 tablespoon raisins

Directions:

Cut avocados in half lengthwise, remove seeds, and set aside.
Scoop pulp from shells and mash smoothly with a spoon. Add
honey to taste and stir in the cream, milk, and raisins. Put into
a serving bowl, return seeds to the pulp, cover tightly with plastic wrap and chill before serving. Recipe serves 4 to 6 people.

Notee: The seeds in the puree are supposed to keep the avocado
from discoloring.

Awesome Honey Pecan Pie

Courtesy of Benefits of Honey, the number one ranked
website on the health benefits of honey
www.benefits-of-honey.com

Ingredients:

¼ pound butter
1 cup sugar
3 eggs, beaten
½ cup corn syrup
½ cup honey
½ teaspoon vanilla
½ teaspoon lemon juice
1-2 cups chopped or whole pecans
1 pinch cinnamon
1 pinch nutmeg (optional, for a more exotic aroma)
9-inch uncooked pie shell

Directions:

Preheat oven to 325°F. In a heavy-bottomed saucepan, brown
butter over medium-high heat to get a nice nutty aroma for the
pie (be careful not to burn it). Remove and allow to cool slightly.
In a large mixing bowl, combine sugar, eggs, syrup, and honey.
Using a wire whisk, blend all ingredients well. Add the browned
butter, vanilla, lemon juice, and pecans. Season with cinnamon
and nutmeg. Continue to whip until all ingredients are well
blended. Pour into pie shell and bake on center rack of oven for
45 minutes to an hour. Remove and allow to cool before serving.

Strawberry Honey Ice Cream

Reprinted with permission by the American Beekeeping
Federation (ABF)

Ingredients:

4 eggs
2¼ cups honey
4 cups milk
2 cups heavy cream
2 cups evaporated milk
1 teaspoon salt
2 tablespoons vanilla
2 cups crushed strawberries
A few whole strawberries, for garnish
Fresh mint, for garnish

Directions:

In a large mixing bowl, beat eggs until uniform and gradually add honey, mixing well. Add milk, cream, evaporated milk,
salt, and vanilla. Mix all ingredients together. Put in ice cream
freezer and once cream is firm (or after about 15 minutes),
add crushed strawberries. Continue to freeze ice cream until
firm. Put in container and set in freezer for three or four hours.
Serve with a fresh strawberry and a sprig of mint to finish.

Honey Apricot Bread

Reprinted with permission by the American Beekeeping
Federation (ABF)

Ingredients:

3 cups flour
3 teaspoons baking powder
½ teaspoon salt
1 teaspoon cinnamon
¼ teaspoon nutmeg
1¼ cups milk
1 cup honey
1 egg, slightly beaten
2 tablespoons coconut oil or canola oil
1 cup chopped dried apricots, soaked in very hot water for 20-
30 minutes

Directions:

In a large bowl, stir together flour, baking powder, salt, cinnamon, and nutmeg. In a separate bowl, combine milk, honey,
eggs, and oil; pour over dry ingredients and stir just enough to
dampen flour. Drain apricots and gently fold into batter. Pour
into buttered loaf pan and bake in a 350°F oven for 60-70 minutes, or until done. Remove from pan. Serve with cream cheese
spread.

Resources

American Institute for Cancer Research
www.aicr.org

Bees-And-Beekeeping.com
www.bees-and-beekeeping.com

Benefits of Honey
www.benefits-of-honey.com

Health Benefits of Honey
www.health-benefits-of-honey.com

HoneyO
www.honeyo.com

The National Honey Board
www.honey.com

Produce for Better Health Foundation (PBH)
www.pbhfoundation.org

The World's Healthiest Foods
www.whfoods.com

Also in the *Farmstand Favorites* Series:

Farmstand Favorites: Apples
978-1-57826-358-5

Farmstand Favorites: Berries
978-1-57826-375-2

Farmstand Favorites: Cheese & Dairy
978-1-57826-395-0

Farmstand Favorites: Garlic
978-1-57826-405-6

Farmstand Favorites: Maple Syrup
978-1-57826-369-1

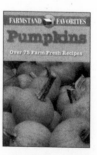

Farmstand Favorites: Pumpkins
978-1-57826-357-8

My Recipes

My Recipes

My Recipes

My Recipes

_____

_____

_____

_____

_____

_____

_____

_____

_____

_____

_____

_____

_____

_____

_____

_____

_____

_____

_____

_____

_____

_____

My Recipes

My Recipes

My Recipes

My Recipes

My Recipes

My Recipes